If No One's Looking, Do We **Have** to Try as Hard?

And other ponderings of women over fifty

Mary Hemlepp

iUniverse, Inc.
Bloomington

If No One's Looking, Do We Have to Try as Hard?
And other ponderings of women over fifty

iUniverse books may be ordered through booksellers or by contacting:

iUniverse
1663 Liberty Drive
Bloomington, IN 47403
www.iuniverse.com
1-800-Authors (1-800-288-4677)

ISBN: 978-1-4620-7345-0 (sc)
ISBN: 978-1-4620-7346-7 (hc)
ISBN: 978-1-4620-7347-4 (e)

Library of Congress Control Number: 2011962315

Printed in the United States of America

iUniverse rev. date: 1/04/2011

Contents

Introduction

Age is just a number.
You're only as old as you feel.
We're not getting older, we're getting better.
Age is a state of mind.
It's better than the alternative.

Most of us over fifty have heard these platitudes offered up by friends trying to make us feel better about aging. I don't know about you, but they don't really work for me. I know how old I am and how society views my age. I recently read that people in my age bracket are now called "near old." I'd like to offer my thanks to the smart aleck who coined that term. The point is, whatever we're called, we're not young any more.

When I was young, it seemed the possibilities were endless. After all, I had my whole life ahead of me. But a few years ago while gazing at the Gulf of Mexico, a glaring reality hit me: Most of my life was behind me. This revelation changed my perspective. I started to ask myself a number of questions: Am I doing what I want to do for the rest of my life? If not, what do I want to do? Am I brave enough to try something new? Why do I feel the need to? Should I take on more or start cutting back? Are there things I want to try that I've never done or used to do, and for some reason, stopped? Am I overreacting about this age thing?

As a product of journalism school with a need to know what people think and why, I asked other women if they felt the same way. When I began to talk informally to friends, I found my feelings were very common among women my age. I also found that women like to talk about this subject. So I conducted an online survey and many interviews with female friends, family, and total strangers who were over fifty.

The online survey was conducted via Survey Monkey in early 2010. It was sent to sixty-three women I knew in three states who were asked to take the survey and forward it to female friends and relatives over age fifty. From years of conducting qualitative and quantitative research in my business, I knew the prospects of getting a good response from an online survey were slim. My hope was that by asking women I knew to participate, and asking them to ask their friends, my chances for a decent response rate would be better than normal. I was right. When the results finally stopped trickling in there were 264 responses from women in twenty-four states. Now I had the push I needed to get to work. The research is not scientific, but it is interesting and provides some insight into how some women over fifty view the world and their place in it.

As I interviewed women, I heard great stories that needed to be told. So, in the second section of this book, you'll read about amazing women who beat the odds, dared to be different, or broke the mold. Some names have been changed throughout to preserve the privacy of the women who shared their stories. Their stories are no less significant because of it.

This book is a snapshot of how some women over fifty feel about themselves and the changes they've been through or are going through as they age. The title comes from a comment about women becoming invisible as we age.

Chapter 1
HAPPY DAYS

At what age are we happiest? Some women say their fifties are or were the happiest time in their lives. There's a peace within and renewed focus on priorities. It's possible this happens because about this time in life, children leave the nest and women have more time for themselves. Many also say by this stage of their lives they care less about what others think of them, and they are more content overall.

In my online survey, 41 percent said they are very happy, and 54 percent said they are mostly happy. Only 4 percent said they are unhappy or not very happy. Given the number of ads for antidepressants and all the turmoil surrounding menopause, this surprised me. Could all these women be on medication? How else can we explain all this happiness? Aren't older women supposed to be unhappy because they're losing their youthful glow and have become empty nesters? This is apparently not true for all women over fifty.

As it turns out, researchers have been asking people over fifty about their happiness for years and found that older people really are happier than younger folks. Gallup did a survey of more than 340,000 Americans in 2008 that showed at around age fifty, people start to worry less and their stress levels become lower. So could this finding make us more eager to grow older? I doubt it. But it is a huge contrast to what we see in the media, which focuses on youth and beauty. Turns out, it's very stressful being young, beautiful, and married while trying to raise 2.5 children.

In 2005, Pew Research Center also measured happiness and found that only one-third of Americans said they were very happy. Like the Gallup survey, this one showed that older people were happier than younger ones. The Pew survey suggested that happiness levels are tied to life events and personality characteristics such as optimism and high self-esteem. This is interesting because many women I know or have talked to as part of this research have family issues such as drugs, divorce, illness, and financial problems. Some talked about low self-esteem and low self-confidence issues they've dealt with throughout their lives. Yet, most of those who responded to the survey said they were happy. Maybe it's because they also said they were realistic or optimistic. More than half said they were realistic. They acknowledged that sometimes things happen and said they dealt with them and moved on. Some 46 percent of survey participants said they were optimists.

Here's more optimism. Even though all of the research participants were over age fifty, nearly half said they felt the best was yet to come in their lives. About 35 percent said they felt like they were treading water trying to decide what to do with the next chapter in their lives. This seems like an optimistic attitude as well. It indicates this group feels it has more to do but hasn't yet decided what that is. When people realize most of their years are behind them, they sometimes feel a sense of urgency to do something new or different with the time they have left. After age fifty is the time of life when many women can devote more hours to volunteering or getting involved in projects they've put off. For some, it's a time to try something they've thought about for years.

Only 18 percent said they'd reached the high point of their lives and were on the downside. It's easy to see where this attitude comes from. Some women's lives have been focused on child rearing, and when the kids leave the nest, it's a letdown for some moms. Most of us want to feel needed, so when kids move out, a big part of our sense of being needed leaves with them. This causes the sadness and loss that some people feel. Women are more susceptible to it, but men are not immune.

Maybe these moms should cheer up. Over the last several years, a new phenomenon has developed. Many kids come home after college and live with their parents until well into their thirties. These so called boomerang kids want the limited responsibility of childhood and the privileges of adulthood, according to Psychology Today.com. Is this really what we want for our kids? Don't we want them to leave the nest and start feathering one of their own? Young adults need to learn to be independent and self-sufficient. What if you got run over by a bus tomorrow? Wouldn't you want your children to know how to live on their own without you? For some moms, it seems the need to be needed outweighs what's really best for their children. It may not seem like it, but Junior can learn to balance his checkbook or his online account without you.

A few more thoughts about happiness and growing older: in interviews and informal discussions with women over fifty, I learned that many of them felt pressured to reinvent themselves or to do more with their lives. Pop culture and media push these ideas. It's not enough that a woman had a satisfying career and wants to enjoy her retirement by gardening, spending time with grandchildren, or traveling with friends. A constant barrage of magazine articles and talk show guests extol the virtues of starting a business, returning to school, or making some other type of big change later in life. That's all fine if you really want to do that, but we need to understand that not everyone wants to start over. It makes me wonder if as a society, we somehow missed the point of women's liberation. Wasn't the whole idea that women could do or be whatever they wanted, including a stay-at-home mom or grandma?

Case in point: my friend Tina was downsized in her early fifties from a company she'd worked for her entire career. Although she missed not going to work every morning and seeing her co-workers, the biggest challenge she had was trying to get past the feeling that she needed to be doing something more. She said this was reinforced in the media to the point her self-esteem began to suffer. She spent the next couple of years looking for the next stage in her life. She tried part-time jobs in fields outside her comfort zone. She read self-help books. She went to therapy. After more than two years, she started to become at peace with herself and realized she didn't have to be anything other than what she wanted to be. Even though she says she's come to terms with her age and her life, some days I'm not so sure.

Another friend who left her job at a younger age by choice had similar feelings. Jan worked for a high-profile politician. In her late forties she remarried and left her job so she could spend more time with her grandchildren. As many of us do at this age, she decided it was time to join a gym. The membership application asked for the name of her employer. No longer having a job, she wrote N/A in the blank. Talk about packing a wallop.

"I'm so much more than N/A," she said.

Another example of the stress caused by expectations we put on ourselves comes from my friend Charlotte. At fifty-four, she said she's the happiest she's ever been, but it hasn't been easy for her to get there. Her big obstacle was not early retirement. It was her perception that her career had not progressed to where she wanted it to be by age fifty.

"I think I would have thrived following a traditional retirement in which I could have actually received a pension and benefits for many years of education and hard work; I would have felt validated and fulfilled," she said.

Instead, at fifty, Charlotte became painfully aware that her dream career was not going to be realized. Not until then did Charlotte realize that her success as a woman and human being did not depend on others' opinions of her and career rewards. Though jobless, she was fortunate to have a working husband to provide for her so that she could start the mental healing process for herself while taking care of the physical and emotional needs of her ailing mother and best friend.

"Being unsuccessful in the business world was actually a gift," Charlotte said. "If I had not lost the many tenured professorship opportunities that I worked so hard for and truly felt I deserved, I would have lost something far more precious: the opportunity to attend to the needs of my mother."

After her mother passed on, Charlotte began seeing a counselor to help her deal with this new loss and to guide her on a path toward self-awareness. Though the healing and growth have been slow, Charlotte feels that she's finally learning that she doesn't need career success or even the approval of others for validation.

She began focusing on reinventing herself by rediscovering the things that once were important to her before she embarked on a career. For example, Charlotte wrote and published a children's book. It was a project that had been on the back burner during all of those years of working toward career success. Publishing it also allowed her to fulfill a promise to her mother.

"This is not some beautiful end to the story," she said. "Life is tough and unfair. I have my ups and downs. I still struggle with self-esteem issues and depression. But I have learned that we can't resign ourselves to failure when life doesn't deal us a fair hand. I have to pull myself up every day to keep from drowning in the mire. I can't say that I'm soaring with the eagles, but I do think I can finally say, after fifty years, that I'm learning to sprout my wings."

In talking to women about their happiness and attitude toward life, it's easy to see that many suffered from a lack of self-confidence when they were young. But as they've grown older, for many their self-confidence has improved and they are more comfortable with themselves. Many more are trying to be. The big question is: What does it take to make us happy and comfortable with ourselves?

In researching this topic of self-confidence in women over fifty I read numerous conflicting articles. Some said women over fifty are more self-confident than younger women whereas other publications said women near retirement age lose confidence. I ran across information that helped clarify some of the discrepancies. For example, self-esteem and self-confidence are not the same thing. Someone may be confident enough to go on stage and do stand-up comedy, but offstage she may believe she is not worthy of success. Self-esteem is about the respect and regard we have for ourselves, and it seems women in general sometimes don't like themselves very much. We don't feel worthy of love, success, or happiness. We feel we could and should be better moms, wives, co-workers, and friends. We see small failures as indictments of our entire being. Just because the flambé flopped doesn't mean we've failed as humans, but we women sometimes take these little blips as total failure.

So, maybe it's about the pursuit of perfection, which no one will ever reach. And yet, we try. We spend thousands trying to look a certain way. We feel we need to drive the right car or live in the right neighborhood. Our kids need to go to the best schools. Do you see a pattern here? Why do we have this need to project a certain image about ourselves? We are projecting perfection while inside we still feel inadequate. Are we really just trying to keep up with the Joneses to make ourselves feel better? Why is it so important what others think about us? Shouldn't we be more focused on trying to like ourselves?

We aren't necessarily born with self-confidence, but it is something we can learn. I'm not very good at trying to fool myself or rationalize a reaction to a situation, so a lot of the techniques I see that are supposed to improve self-esteem and confidence don't work for me. I do believe in trying to replace negative thoughts with positive ones. Negativism is an easy trap to fall into, especially if those around us are negative. I'm not suggesting we all become like Pollyanna, but we can be happier if we start looking for the good in our lives, being more aware of the positives, and spending more time with upbeat people.

I believe that each of us is in charge of her own happiness. No one else can make us happy over the long term. We must like ourselves and focus on peace and contentment. So many people think material things will make them happy. Fill in the blank here: If only I had _____, I could be happy. Really? Think about it again. Why is that so important to you? Why would it make you happier? Would that happiness last hours, days, or a lifetime? Although money can make life easier, and we all feel better knowing we can pay our bills on time, having more money to buy more stuff doesn't seem to be the answer. Researchers from several universities have found that experiences make us happier than things do. That's probably because we share experiences with others, which gives us good memories.

Being happy and content with life is a goal. No one is happy all the time, but if we realize what it is within us that produces happiness, contentment, and peace of mind, then we can strive to achieve that each day. The first step is to realize that we have to take each day as it comes versus thinking our happiness as a whole is wrapped up in what happens today.

Chapter 2
AGING BEAUTY QUEENS, SEX SYMBOLS, AND THE REST OF US

For some women, being overachievers in the classroom or the office has boosted their self-confidence. Others have sought fulfillment through the successes of their children or their husbands' careers. And some have relied on their looks. But as we all learn at some point in our lives, there's always someone smarter, wealthier, or prettier. This is a harder lesson for some than for others.

By the time we reach our fifties, the happiness and self-confidence of some women are affected by health issues or the realization that we no longer look twenty-five. This is especially difficult for those we see suffering from "aging beauty queen syndrome." Although not a real disease, this syndrome affects a lot of women. You know who they are. They were the popular girls in high school and college. The ones all the girls wanted to be friends with and all the boys wanted to date. And, oh yeah, they looked terrific in anything, especially jeans and swimsuits. For many, those days are long past, and for the most part, the former hotties look a lot like the rest of us now —a little heavier, a little wrinkled, and a little gray (underneath our fabulous hair color).

But some can't give it up. They tend to dress too provocatively. Their hair is a little too big, too blonde, or too dark. Instead of believing less is more, they use more makeup in hope of camouflaging their wrinkles. You've seen this. The makeup settles in the wrinkles and makes them look even worse. So much for aging gracefully. Some baby boomers are fighting it tooth and nail, while others are enjoying the freedom that comes with age.

What about Hollywood's sex symbols? How do they handle getting older? Women like Jacqueline Bissett, Cher, Bo Derek, and Raquel Welch? Who could forget Raquel Welch in the animal skin bikini? Every teenage boy of that era probably had the poster, and every teenage girl and her mother wanted to look like Raquel.

So, how *do* these and other former sex symbols handle aging? Mostly with surgery, I'd guess from what I see on TV. Some are very open about the procedures they've had, and others want us to pretend not to notice. Some, however, seem to have accepted aging as part of life. Some admit to their surgical procedures at an earlier stage of life and now say they regret having had them. Others talk about how fans are somehow let down to see their sex symbols as older women. Several have on gone on TV recently with no makeup so the rest of us won't feel so bad. In an appearance on a daytime talk show, a former sex symbol who was sixty-nine at the time, said of getting older, "It's a bitch." Ain't that the truth?

As difficult as aging is for the beauty queens and sex symbols of the world, it's no easier for the rest of us. Ads for diet products, wrinkle creams, and goofy exercise gadgets fill the airwaves and pages of magazines. Here we are, over fifty and trying to recapture our youth from a jar, or in most cases, many jars, tubes, and bottles. Did you know there's actually a product called "Hope in a Jar"?

I suspect my bathroom cabinets look a lot like yours. They're full of products we use and many more we've been disappointed with that are now sitting there aging just like we are. How many thousands of dollars must we have spent to recapture the youthful look we now so badly want? And as for diet and exercise regimen, many of us give it the old college try, but don't stay with it.

According to my survey, nearly half the respondents said they try to exercise regularly and eat a healthy diet, but more than half have gained nearly twenty pounds or more since age thirty-five. The upside of this is the other half have not, and even a few, 6 percent, said they weigh less. Almost 62 percent said they look OK for their age, and a quarter of them said they think they look good. Only 12.5 percent said they think they look old and tired.

Are you as surprised as I am to learn this? When I get together with friends, the conversation invariably turns to age, weight, sagging skin (and other things), and all the aches and pains of growing older. From the conversations I've been privy to, I'd never have guessed any of my friends would say they think they look good or even OK for their age. We talk about how fat we are, how we can never find clothes that look good on us, how we need plastic surgery, and how generally unattractive we've become. We negatively feed off one another and the comments get so bad that you'd think you're sitting with a table full of women who look like the Wicked Witch of the West.

Do the survey findings mean our friends say one thing but believe another? Maybe they just mean we all need someone to compliment us occasionally. Maybe if we tell our friends how bad we think we look, they'll tell us we don't. I'm not a psychiatrist, so I don't know if that's the case. I'm just sayin'.

One research study I ran across showed that women investors and owners of small businesses were more likely to feel youthful. As a small business owner, some days I'm not sure I'd agree. When I look at the youthfulness of my clients and younger practitioners in my field, I sometimes feel pretty old. In general, most people my age say they can't believe how old they actually are. In their heads, they're thin, beautiful, and twenty-five.

But in reality we are over fifty, for whatever that's worth. A friend recently told me that once you're past fifty, you become invisible. She believes we're no longer attractive to the opposite sex, and no one pays much attention to us anymore. As someone who always liked attention, she's disappointed about this. On the other hand, she believes it's freeing.

"If no one's looking, maybe we don't have to try so hard," she said.

On one social networking site, women were discussing how to fit in with younger co-workers. Some talked about how frustrated or hurt they've been by colleagues who are decades younger than they are. Others gave tips about what not to say, how to text, and said that wearing a watch is so 1990s. Others said they weren't too concerned about fitting in. One said males and younger colleagues tune her out, so since she's invisible she doesn't worry about fitting in. She does her job and everyone's happy. That may work for her, but I'm not sure about the majority of us.

I hadn't noticed being ignored in public places until a friend mentioned it. But soon after, I started paying attention to how my friends and I were treated in restaurants. On several occasions, servers didn't seem to be as interested in us as they were in tables of men or couples. In one restaurant, a friend and I were completely ignored by our server. He seemed almost angry that we'd stopped in for lunch.

On another occasion, at dinner with two friends, we were totally ignored by a young, cute, female server. I complimented her dress and tried to be friendly, but she was totally uninterested in giving our table good service. Right behind us was a table of two couples, and we noticed she was extremely attentive to their needs, while we had to wave her down to ask for a simple coffee refill.

One of my friends summed it up this way: "Restaurants and bars want a young, attractive clientele. We don't fit that profile, so we are a deterrent to bringing in those customers. When younger people see us eating there, they think the place is not hip and find 'younger' places to hang out."

This poor treatment of mature women was fascinating to me, and the idea that no one wants to serve us because we look a certain way also was interesting. You'd think that women in their fifties and sixties would be good tippers because many have a good deal of disposable income. I wondered what professional servers think about mature women, so my son, who has worked as a server, helped me out with this one. Here are some of the answers from his friends:

- Large groups of women are boisterous and obnoxious. They disturb the people around them with their "cackling" so servers want to get them out quickly.

- Most don't tip well.

- When a server approaches and there are multiple conversations going on, the server feels like he or she is interrupting. Sometimes the women seem frustrated that the server is there to take their order.

- Older women sometimes are demanding and don't treat servers with respect.

- Older women linger too long after they've paid their checks, taking up a table that could be given to others. Servers resent this because it keeps them from getting new clients and more tips.

Ouch! It doesn't sound as if we're invisible at all. Maybe we're loud because we're being ignored? What is it about women of a certain age when we go out in groups? Are we feeling free to be ourselves no matter what others around us think? Do we have to talk louder to be heard over some in the group who won't stop talking? Are we poor tippers because servers ignore us?

Whatever the reason, mature women are hard to ignore. We're everywhere, taking part in everything. There's no doubt women over fifty today are different in many ways from those of our mothers' and grandmothers' generations. We certainly look different. No longer do we cut our hair short and get a tight, curly perm or put it in a bun. One huge difference is the absence of gray hair. Hair color may be the one thing that's changed our looks the most. I've recently heard that gray hair is in. Well, just because some fashion guru declares it so doesn't mean it will happen. I, for one, am not giving in to gray, and I'll bet you aren't, either.

We dress differently from the women before us, too. We wear jeans and T-shirts, sweats, and athletic shoes, instead of housedresses and stockings. We don't worry, as my grandmother did, about the color we wear being too bright for older women; we just worry about the color looking good on us. I distinctly remember a shopping trip with my mother and my dad's mother. My mother noticed a dress in a beautiful deep rose color and pointed it out to my grandmother, saying it would it look nice with her skin tone. My grandmother was mortified. She said something like: "Honey, I'm an old woman and I can't wear a color that bright." Would any of us ever think that way today?

Another big change for women of today is working outside the home. Many of us are and have been for years. Some aren't even looking forward to retirement, and others have started a second career after retirement. Recent news stories point to the graying of the American workforce. People are working longer for several reasons. We're in better health today because of advances in health care and less physically demanding jobs. Downsizing, however, has created a group of fifty- and sixty-something workers who are finding they're overqualified for the jobs that are available. For many, the financial need to continue working is pressing. Losses in the stock market and other economic issues have forced older workers to continue working past retirement age.

As for better health, we exercise in gyms, take dance classes, bike, and try things we've put off for years. A couple of years ago, I decided to take horseback riding lessons. Some of my friends were amazed because I'm not particularly athletic or outdoorsy. I think secretly they were afraid I'd fall off a horse and break a hip. We didn't see our mothers and grandmothers do such things as they aged. Although they worked hard for hearth and home, they were much less independent, and many weren't as driven to try new things. That could be because they were so busy trying to pay the bills and keep the housework done that they didn't have time to try new things.

The bottom line is that there's no easy stereotype when it comes to women over fifty, and I think that's a good thing. Maybe we're finally realizing one size doesn't fit all and that's OK.

Chapter 3
HEALTHY, WEALTHY, AND WISE

How are you? It's a simple question we ask people every day. More than half the survey respondents said they feel OK most days and 44 percent said they feel great. This aligns with what I hear and see day to day. Most of my friends are healthy and few have suffered from serious illness or disease. But I know many others are faced with illness, and some have passed on at an early age.

When it comes to exercise, most of us have tried it, but very few are able to make it a regular part of our lives. We join gyms and immediately become intimidated by the equipment and by others' young, toned bodies. We even join with our friends thinking we'll motivate each other, but mostly, we find excuses not to work out and end up going to lunch instead.

We buy exercise equipment to use at home, thinking that will be easier and less intimidating than going to the gym. But how often do we really use the equipment? If yours is like mine, it's mostly a dust catcher. I also have a nice collection of exercise DVDs that are rarely used. There's really no excuse for not working out. I'm just lazy.

Not all of us are slackers, though. Juanita, a retired teacher, told me a story about exercise and women over fifty. Juanita always loved to dance, but never took lessons when she was a child. In her twenties, she decided to take up belly dancing. Now in her late fifties, Juanita is teaching belly dancing—and not just to young women. Some of her students are in their eighties. She said the key to exercise is making it fun, so she and her students don't take themselves too seriously. Juanita also works part-time at a gym that caters to older folks, the oldest of which is ninety-nine.

Since we go through different phases of life, I wanted to know how women feel about themselves now versus when they were younger. So I asked how their lives are different now than they were twenty years ago. Many, as you might expect, said they have more time to focus on themselves because their children are now adults. This was an open-ended question, so the answers varied, but the theme of having grown children was woven throughout. Some women enjoy the freedom, and others are looking for something to fill the void. Some said they enjoy the slower pace, which makes them feel more relaxed and happy. Some also said they are more secure financially, which gives them peace of mind.

Although not everyone is financially secure and many lost thousands in the stock market downturn, women over fifty have strong influence over household purchases and enormous buying power. As someone whose career is public relations and marketing, I've long had an interest in the buying power of women and have done some research about it.

Over the years, trends have changed and now women are considered the chief purchasing officers in about 80 to 85 percent of homes, depending on which survey you read. The influence of women is seen not only in typical female-oriented purchases like appliances and other household items, but also in the purchase of cars and electronics, which used to be the domain of men.

Most of this change has occurred because more women are in the workplace today than their counterparts of the 1950s and '60s. We really have come a long way, baby. An argument can be made that there's still inequality in some areas, but when it comes to spending power the research proves women are the ones marketers should be seeking.

As we age, this group is no less powerful. Here's a fact from Mass Mutual Financial Group (2007): women age fifty and older control a net worth of $19 trillion and own more than three-fourths of the nation's financial wealth. You read that right—trillion with a "T." Even in this recessionary age, statistics show that women are generating and controlling more wealth than ever before. Additionally, in January 2010 more women than men were in the workforce, according to US Labor Department statistics for that month.

Although we are more financially independent than generations before us, we still suffer from the loss of our spouses and have concerns about job loss. Some women have suffered from divorce or are grieving the death of a spouse, and this has resulted in a life that is very different in many aspects. Others are getting used to retirement or having a retired spouse, while some are dealing with the loss of a job they thought they'd retire from.

Several said their jobs are keeping them busier and others who weren't working twenty years ago are working now. According to one respondent: "I'm busier professionally at age sixty-six and less busy with raising children and/or grandchildren."

I interviewed Angie about the changes in her life over the last twenty years or more. Angie's a retired teacher and artist in her late fifties and splits her time between Kentucky and California. As a younger woman, Angie felt driven to be independent and have a career, but also felt the need to be a mother, which she is.

She grew up in Kentucky and was expected to get married and live the country club lifestyle. So she got married, "dressed right, went to the right church, lived in the right neighborhood," and generally did what was expected of her. Later she moved to California and continued teaching and pursuing her art. She still spends part of the year there to be close to her grandchildren. After she retired from teaching, Angie felt the need to do something new, but wasn't sure what that was. During a visit to Kentucky, she and two younger male friends decided to start a retail business.

"I thought to myself, if not now, when?" she said. "People were appalled because I was risking my safety net. But really, there is no safety net. I've never been a business person, but now, at this age, I can say I've done it. I'm proud of it."

She believes that if there's something you want to do, do it now. She's not alone in this belief. One respondent said: "I'm much more aware of appreciating every day and trying to make the most of everything." Another said she is "on the brink of a major life change (something I just feel) but I have no idea what it is."

Some women said they enjoy the wisdom and freedom that comes with maturity. Here are a few of their comments.

- "I am wiser. More content with what I have. Not so uptight."

- "I know how much I don't know, but it does not bother me. I care much less about what people think."

- "I accept myself with all the warts. Don't sweat the small stuff. Greater insight and wisdom."

- "I have goals now."

- "I am more content."

- "I realize how quickly life can change and make the most of each day."

- "I know what I want and what I am doing."

- "I think that I am more confident than I was when I was younger."

- "I am more confident, comfortable, and expressive now than I was twenty years ago."

- "I am far more secure, confident, spiritual, and productive."

- "I'm more focused on others rather than [having the] 'it's all about me mentality' I had twenty years ago."

- "I know clearly what is important and what is not."

- "I'm older, a little wiser, more tolerant, more loving."

- "I feel like I have more control over my life and what happens to me."

But not all the survey respondents were upbeat about this stage of their lives. Some have health issues and others don't have the energy they used to have. Some say they have financial problems and are suffering because of the loss of a job or a loved one. Others are lonely, and their life experiences have made some cynical. In the words of one respondent: "Aging sucks."

Although most women are not happy about the aging process, they do have life experiences they can pass along to younger women. In asking survey participants what advice they would offer, there was one overriding theme: get an education so you can support yourself. Many mature women have learned they can't depend on others for happiness, so several respondents said younger women should do what makes them happy. They also would tell younger women to enjoy every second of life because it passes by quickly, to have a dream and follow it, and to "be who you are."

Respondents advised younger women to take some time for themselves, focus on health and fitness, and not be afraid to ask for advice. Family and good friends were important to a large number of respondents. One suggested keeping good friends close because they become more important as we age. This is good advice because people who have a network of good friends live longer. According to one study, it is even more important than having close family relationships. Younger people have learned this in recent years as more have moved away from home for their careers and have new "families" of friends.

Socializing as we age has a positive effect on health, especially in lowering stress levels, fighting depression, and keeping blood pressure down. In many instances, spending time with friends can even help nutrition and brain function because some mature women who live alone don't eat right. So, in addition to the strong emotional support friends offer, they also can be good for your health.

Women who responded to my survey said friends were important to them. Eighty percent said their friends play a very important role in their lives. Nearly 30 percent said they see or talk with close friends daily or nearly every day. Half said weekly.

Sandy, who's in her late sixties, told me she had three or four close friends who were vital to her life. Years earlier when she was going through a divorce, she socialized with other women who were in the same situation even though they had little else in common.

Several women said they have a close network of friends, and some are trying to rekindle friendships from childhood. In some cases, it's working out well. Use of social media among women over fifty continues to increase, and some said they've reconnected with classmates through Facebook. For others, reconnecting has not been so successful. After the "remember when" conversations, many decided they had little left in common with childhood friends.

One question I didn't ask, but wish I had, is whether the respondents had a best friend. I'm not sure I ever had one best friend. I've always had several friends and considered many on the best-friend level. I think some people are more comfortable with having a best friend with whom they share everything. As I've spoken with women for this book, I've found that most are very open and eager to share their thoughts, their lives, and their dirty laundry. Maybe it's easier for some people to tell a stranger their secrets.

In addition to building good friendships and taking some time for themselves, the older women offered other advice to younger women, including the following:

- "When you come to a big stumbling block in the road (and you will), remind yourself that five years from now it will just be a pebble—keep on going."

- "Keep a sense of humor, and having it all isn't as great as it sounds!"

- "Enjoy each day of your life. Be positive and look forward to your older age. Life will be great if you do."

- "Stay active, stay positive! Don't strive for perfection, but be your best."

- "Enjoy your children while they are young because they can move far away and not come home."

- "Plan for the future. Take care of your own finances, and be involved in it [your finances] daily."

- "Live your life with integrity; be honest with yourself and others. Be yourself and don't worry so much what others think. Know your limits."

- "Read, read, read. It is not a luxury to drink coffee and read the newspaper—it is a necessity."

- "Appreciate where you are in life."

- "If you have a chance to do something you really want to do, don't pass up the chance. It may never come your way again."

- "Don't ever settle or live with things that make you unhappy."

- "Live, don't simply exist."

- "Enjoy the different stages in your life because none last forever."

My friend Elizabeth grew up in West Virginia. She was a self-described control freak who now believes that part of her personality came from insecurity.

Like many people, she's had some setbacks along the way, including losing a child. Her mother, who's a spirited lady now in her eighties, gave Elizabeth some advice during the dark days after the death of her baby. Her mother told Elizabeth she had to learn that sometimes we have no control. But here's the really good advice: "You have to learn to go with the flow and embrace change." Although it wasn't easy, Elizabeth said that after she was able to heed her mother's advice, her life has been easier.

"There's freedom in reflection," she said. "I look back and see how things changed in my life and where that led."

Here are a few more thoughts about change and insecurity. We shouldn't be afraid to try something new. One of the biggest frustrations I have with some women is that they settle. They get comfortable, even if they aren't totally satisfied. And a large number of them are afraid of change. Many have the mindset of "it's good enough for me" instead of thinking how the situation could be better. I believe it all goes back to the self-confidence issue. We don't believe we can do better or deserve better, so it becomes a self-fulfilling prophecy. Life's too short to be unhappy, and we have to be less afraid of change. Change is inevitable so we have to take control of the things we can change, and learn how to react to those things we can't change. Remember the Serenity Prayer?

Chapter 4
WHAT? ME WORRY?

Although many of us have myriad concerns about aging, we have other worries as well. One survey answer summed it all up for many women: "What doesn't worry me?" A few of the women who took the online survey said they don't really worry, but do have concerns about certain things. One said not worrying was a choice she's made. Another said she doesn't worry about things over which she has no control.

The number one answer to the open-ended question about what women over fifty worry about was their children and grandchildren. I doubt anyone is surprised by that. We worry about their health, their finances, and their overall happiness. The survey also reflects some differences about the types of worry we have about children. When they are young adults, we tend to focus our worry on their success in college, and on whether they will be financially independent, happy people. As our children get older and have children of their own, our worry refocuses to include things like what kind of world our grandchildren will inherit.

One surprise for me in the research was that a little more than half of the women I surveyed said they did not have grandchildren. Again, this may not be indicative of women our age as a whole. It might only be those who opted to take the survey. Of those who did have grandchildren, 31 percent said they see them or talk to them often. I don't have grandchildren, but I seem to be surrounded by friends and family who do, and they are very involved in their lives. For some, their grandchildren are like their second generation of children. Some babysit regularly, some travel out of town for long periods of time to visit them, and some are raising their grandchildren for various reasons.

Then there are those who are caring for children and/or grandchildren and aging parents. MSNBC.com said in a 2007 story that twenty million Americans were struggling to care for aging parents while raising their families. At about the same time, the Pew Research Center said about one in eight Americans between forty and sixty were part of this sandwich generation. As baby boomers age, this phenomenon is likely to grow. The US Census Bureau projects that by 2030, people over sixty-five will make up about 20 percent of our population.

The concern about health and being taken care of is reflected in the answers to the question about what worries women over 50. An overarching theme was concern about deteriorating health and being able to take care of themselves, both physically and financially, as they age. One woman said her worst fear is she will have to go to a nursing home. Some expressed concern about Alzheimer's disease in their families. One woman said she worries that she'll die alone and die before she's happy. Isn't it sad that someone who has lived more than fifty years hasn't known happiness?

Given that the survey was done during a recession, I asked respondents to take the economy off their list of worries. Based on conversations with friends and family and national polls I'd seen, the economy was on most people's minds. Even though I asked participants to exclude it, several said they could not. One said it would be hard to exclude the economy because it was affecting her family at the time. Another said, "We can't escape the economy. So much depends on it. Retirement. Health care. The future of our children and grandchildren…."

Some said they worry about our country. Several women expressed concerns about the direction in which our country is headed and listed loss of freedom, bitterness that divides us, loss of Social Security, and lack of personal responsibility. A few mentioned war and terrorism.

Several also said they worry about the youth of today because they see a lack of respect and a certain amount of laziness. Others said they worry about the type of nation we are leaving for our young people.

Some said they worry about little things, and others said they don't worry about things they can't change. A few said they don't worry. One respondent said, "I really don't worry very much. Why should I? God said he will take care of his children."

Speaking of faith, how important is that to women over fifty? Ninety percent said it was "Very" or "Somewhat Important," but when asked how often they attended religious services, only 52 percent said "Often." The role of faith in the respondents' lives is not surprising. Most were Southerners, and people in the South normally rank their belief in God and the importance of religion in their lives higher than those in other parts of the country. The Pew Research Center's Forum on Religion and Public Life Survey found that people from Mississippi were the most religious. They ranked highest in the importance of religion, worship attendance, frequency of prayer, and belief in God. The lowest ranking states were Alaska and several in New England.

For many, their faith was related to another survey question: How do you keep a positive outlook as you hear about illness and death of so many around us? Many said their faith in God and the belief in seeing loved ones again help them stay positive. Several mentioned the afterlife in some form and said they use prayer and meditation to cope.

One cancer survivor I interviewed told me her faith had gotten stronger as she's gotten older. This faith doesn't include church. "I believe the type of life I've led is more important than going to church," she said.

Her bout with cancer made her appreciate life more and realize that she's not indestructible. She also believes positive thoughts create good energy, and said she frequently talks to God.

"When I'm going to have a real sit-down conversation with God, I pray in the shower," she said.

Two other women who were present and also being interviewed said they did the same thing. And I always thought the shower was for singing.

For others I've spoken with or who responded to the survey, a sense of optimism and a realistic attitude prevailed. They accept death as a part of life and try to concentrate on living rather than dwelling on the negative. One common theme among this group was that death is out of our control; it's something that happens to everyone, and even though we never forget our loved ones, we have to move on. One said: "What are we going to do? Accept it and go on." Another said when her mother was diagnosed with cancer, her mother viewed it as a phase. Because of that attitude, the respondent said that's the way she'd chosen to view bad news.

Some talked about the importance of exercise in helping keep their minds and bodies strong, and others said they focus on being thankful for what they have. A few wrote about their experiences of recently losing someone and how they are trying to cope. Two or three said they'd never lost anyone close to them and didn't know how they'd handle it.

It seems as we get older, we hear a lot of bad news. When I talk to my mother, many times the conversation is about people who are sick or have recently died. I asked her one day, somewhat jokingly, if she had any healthy friends. I suggested she find some because she needed positivity in her life.

I wondered what motivates women or what they look forward to as they age, so I asked the question on the survey and in interviews. Once again, many mentioned spending time with friends and family. Some said they enjoyed their work and others mentioned their pets. Service or helping others, their faith, exercise, travel, and looking forward to retirement were also popular answers. One respondent said, "Life itself motivates me. I look forward to tomorrow."

Another woman I'll call Ana said her job motivates her. She moved from her home in the Northeast to Florida and has found it difficult to make friends.

"My friends are my co-workers, but many of them are just that. During Thanksgiving and Christmas, they spend it with their own families, and I feel the void since I am so far from home," she said. "I used to be the one that brought the lonely into our home or the home of family members who are the cooks of the family, and the parties are around food. And trust me, Latinos always include dancing at our parties. It is the second main event."

Gina, whose story was told previously regarding her perception that she'd failed in her career, said nothing really motivates her. She said she sets daily goals because she realizes she might not be here tomorrow. "It's a whole sensibility thing," she said.

What about living in the present? Don't you think it's hard to do? It's a goal I've set for myself because I spend a lot of time looking two or three steps down the road and trying to prepare. By doing this, I'm missing out on what's happening to me now. Many people seem to live in the past and dwell on mistakes or other negative things. I try to avoid that because it doesn't accomplish anything other than making me feel bad.

One woman I interviewed said she lives in the present but still spends time making what she hopes are the right decisions for her future.

"I am trying my hardest to make the most money now and make sure I invest in my 401(K). I plan to buy a car in the next three years so that when I retire that will be paid for. My home as well should be paid for. So, I do live in the present thinking about the future, but also enjoy two to three vacations a year."

A friend told me she thinks about the past and is thankful for the present. She said: "I rarely think about the future. I think about death a lot, and feel sadness for my grandchildren. I want them to remember me."

To stop worrying about the future or lamenting the past, we have to learn to live in the present. Research shows people who do this are happier because they are replacing negative thoughts with positive ones. Accepting things you can't change, being thankful for the good things, and minimizing negative thoughts and time spent around negative people tend to improve a person's outlook on life and affect health positively. All of this is easier said than done.

Chapter 5

I AM WOMAN. HEAR ME ROAR.

One theme that I've heard many times through my conversations and interviews is that as women age, we feel more independent. I wonder if this was always so. Women haven't always had the ability to pursue any career path they wanted. Heck, there was a time when we couldn't even have a bank account in our own names or own property. And, oh yes, there was that little thing that happened in 1920 that finally allowed us to vote.

If you consider the choices your mother and your grandmother had, you quickly see they had little independence. My mother and her mother always worked full-time and were very independent. This was a necessity for both, and an anomaly for women of their generations. My grandmother was a single mom most of the time my mother was a child, so she had to work. She worked long, hard hours in retail to pay the bills. My mother worked in the medical field to supplement my dad's income. She couldn't really afford to stay home and bake cookies, or have dinner on the table at 5:00 as so many moms did during the '50s and '60s. But I think that's OK. It never bothered me that she worked and it probably is why I always knew I would. It's also probably why I've always been an independent person.

Even though many women who graduated from high school in the '60s and '70s didn't have a lot of choice about what they'd do with their lives, I always aspired to do something more than get married young and have children. But that's exactly what I did. I was married, had a child, and divorced by my early twenties. I didn't go to college full-time or choose a career until several years later, but it all worked out and probably for the better. Had I gone to college in the '70s with my friends, I'd probably have become a teacher. There's nothing wrong with teaching. It's a noble profession. I just don't think I'd have been very good at it.

Several of my high school friends did go to college in the early and mid-'70s, but I didn't know until recently that one of them was allowed to go on one condition: she had to become a teacher or a nurse. Girls today would laugh at this, but my friend knew her dad was serious. She wanted to get a degree in forestry. Instead, she'll soon retire from teaching.

Another friend, Rebecca, who's in her sixties, grew up in Florida and attended a women's college in Louisiana. When she rushed her sorority, she wore what any appropriate young Southern woman would have worn: a hat, gloves, a girdle, and stockings. As graduation approached, she wore what had become the traditional uniform of young women all over the United States: jeans, a peasant blouse, and no bra. Hers is but one example of how quickly things changed for women during that time. We went from being proper young ladies who did what their fathers told them, to women who wanted equal rights and the ability to take charge of their birth control.

Many women of our generation were the first in their families to earn college degrees. Some went to college to find a husband, but many were excited to embark on a new chapter and have careers—something most of their mothers didn't and couldn't have.

A friend said her son asked her what was the first profession she wanted. This in itself is a huge change from when we were kids. No one would have asked her mother that question. It was assumed that women would grow up to be wives and mothers.

My friend said she clearly remembers thinking she wanted her first job to be cleaning windshields at the gas station because she knew she could do it better than the men who were doing it. For me, it was being an elevator operator. It seemed like fun to open and close those big doors and be the one who knew where everything in the department store was. Maybe she and I didn't have big aspirations, but at least we had some.

In the early '70s, only about 9 percent of college degrees were conferred on women. By 2001, that percentage climbed to 50 percent. Today, more women than men go to college, and in a study released in August 2011, Pew Research Center found that women have a more positive view than men about the value of higher education.

In addition to the fact that many more women today graduate from college than they did when I was young, another major difference is that we mostly had jobs, while they have pursued careers. Even though many women of a certain age have left the workforce, either because they wanted to or because they were forced out, millions are still working. US Department of Labor statistics from 2008, the latest numbers on the website, showed 12.6 million women over age 55 were working. These statistics show the ten leading occupations for women age 55 and over in 2008 were secretaries and administrative assistants (806,000); registered nurses (531,000); elementary and middle school teachers (482,000); bookkeeping, accounting, and auditing clerks (366,000); retail salespersons (355,000); nursing, psychiatric, and home health aides (298,000); cashiers (295,000); maids and housekeepers (275,000);

first-line supervisors/managers of retail sales workers (274,000); and receptionists and information clerks (261,000).

(Source: U.S. Department of Labor, Bureau of Labor Statistics, Employment and Earnings, January 2009 and Current Population Survey, Annual Averages, 2008, unpublished tables.)

In looking at those numbers, there aren't a lot of surprises when it comes to the leading occupations for older women. Even though women still face inequality in pay, the work world has opened up for younger women. For instance, we now face a shortage of nurses because women can go into so many other fields. Many now become doctors instead of nurses. They become lawyers instead of legal secretaries. And they own restaurants instead of just waiting tables.

This leads to another phenomenon for women in the workplace: women are starting their own businesses in droves. Many are looking for work-life balance, and others are tired of adhering to other people's rules and timetables. Women have been working while keeping the home fires burning, so it seems only natural that the next step would be to use those talents for running businesses. The ability to multi-task and compromise along with their more nurturing personalities is what some studies suggest make women good bosses and business owners.

Here are a few statistics taken from the website of the National Association of Women Business Owners. (www.nawbo.org)

Women-Owned Businesses in the United States

- More than 10 million firms are owned by women (50 percent or more), employing more than 13 million people, and generating $1.9 trillion in sales as of 2008.

- Three-quarters of all women-owned businesses are majority owned by women (51percent or more), for a total of 7.2 million firms, employing 7.3 million people, and generating $1.1 trillion in sales.

- Women-owned firms (50 percent or more) account for 40 percent of all privately held firms.

Businesses Owned by Women of Color in the United States

- Nearly two million firms are majority-owned (51 percent or more) by women of color.

- These firms employ 1.2 million people and generate $165 billion in revenues annually.

- Between 2002 and 2008, these firms grew faster than all privately held firms.

Million-Dollar Businesses Owned by Women in the United States

- One in five firms with revenue of $1 million or more is woman-owned.

- Three percent of all women-owned firms have revenues of $1 million or more compared with 6 percent of men-owned firms.

Although two-income families certainly are the norm, and for most, necessary, women's and men's roles have changed dramatically in my lifetime. It's interesting to note that some women in their fifties and beyond say they have felt stifled by husbands who wanted to rule the roost rather than be a good partner. After divorce or death of a spouse, many women feel liberated for the first time. My mother tells stories about friends whose personalities seem to have blossomed after they were on their own. She's been surprised to find out how many women were kept under their husbands' thumbs. These are women mostly in their seventies who grew up in an age when men told women what to do and when to do it.

My friend Adrienne told me about growing up in the South when her mother would dress for dinner and have everything ready and waiting when Adrienne's father got home from work. The interesting twist to the story was that after her father retired, he and Adrienne's mother seemed to switch roles. She began to work full-time and he had dinner ready for her. It's something that Adrienne thought she'd never see.

Women I interviewed talked about how their need for having a man in their life waned as they matured. I asked my friend Carla, who's a family therapist, about this and other aspects of my research. She said some changes in how we feel and what we need are hardwired in our brains, and have been for thousands of years. For example, when we're young, we're looking for a husband who can help us have children. We probably are not even conscious of it, she said. Then as we age and are past child-bearing years, the urge for procreation is gone, and men are no longer as necessary to a happy life. This is not man bashing. Many women have a hard time coping with the loss of the man in their life, and many don't know how they would go on without them. But the dependence on men and the declining need to have a man is a reality for scores of women. It doesn't mean they didn't love their spouses or are happy they're gone. It just means they may not feel a strong need for another one at this time in their lives.

My aunt summed up her thoughts like this: "At my age, men are looking for a nurse or a purse."

She's not totally wrong. My therapist friend, who's in her sixties, said men she's dated asked her early in the relationship about her retirement account and whether she owns her home. Although those relationships didn't get very far, Carla said it's really not surprising that men are interested in these financial matters. Many her age have been through divorce and lost savings, retirement accounts, and homes, so they want to make sure when they get involved again that women they date are financially secure. This is another dramatic cultural change. In years gone by, men would never have openly questioned a woman's financial situation because men viewed it as their job to take care of women.

How they got from there to here: Stories you never knew about the women next door

We're surrounded by women who've done amazing or interesting things. They're not rich or famous. They haven't won a lot of awards, but probably should have. They're regular gals who took whatever life threw at them and made it better. They're the survivors, the pioneers, and the ones we call mom, grandmother, aunt, friend, or neighbor. If you ask them, you'll be amazed at the stories they can tell. Here's what a few of them told me.

Winnie

My mother-in-law was a real-life "Rosie the Riveter." Winnie grew up in a big family in the hills of West Virginia. As the oldest child, she had huge responsibilities to help the family. Many days her mother would give her a choice of either hoeing corn or staying inside to cook and watch the younger kids.

"Sometimes I'd go hoe corn," she said. "But I knew mom wanted a break from the kids and the house, so most of the time I'd cook and watch the little ones."

When she became a teenager, Winnie clearly saw the life ahead of her was that of her mother, and she knew she didn't want it. So she moved in with a family in the city, doing housework and babysitting while attending high school. She became ill and moved in with relatives in the same city and finished high school when she recovered from her illness.

She had a job lined up to begin immediately after graduation, but it wasn't in West Virginia. Unbeknownst to her parents, she'd been hired to work at Willow Run, an airplane factory in Michigan. Her uncle loaned her money for the bus ticket. Before letting her move so far away, her uncle warned of the dangers of the world for a young, naïve girl. But he needn't have worried. Winnie could take care of herself.

Meanwhile, back at Hickory Ridge, Winnie's father told one of her brothers they were going to the city to pick up Winnie and bring her back to the country. The younger brother said, "No need to do that. She's gone." Needless to say, her parents weren't pleased.

In Michigan, after a short stay at a boarding house, she rented a room from two sisters who'd turned their home into a rooming house for young women working at the factory. Winnie worked in the tail of the B-24 Liberator bombers because she was one of the few people small enough to fit in the cramped space. She has vivid memories of the experience and talks about seeing Henry Ford, who built the plant on farmland he owned. Thousands of people worked at the plant, which in 1944 produced 650 B-24s per month.

Winnie's adventure lasted less than a year, but it was a life-changing experience for the young woman from the country. She was always independent, but moving to Michigan allowed her to see things she'd never seen before and meet a lot of new people, including her future husband.

While waiting for a bus to take her back to Michigan after a holiday break, she met a former Marine named Charlie. He also worked at the Willow Run factory because he couldn't find work near his home in Kentucky. A few weeks after meeting the two were married at the boarding house where Winnie lived. Her landladies even made the wedding cake.

As the war began to wind down, Winnie and Charlie were eager to start a more normal life together and moved back to his hometown in Kentucky. He eventually went to college using his veteran's benefits. She had three babies and was a stay-at-home mom for several years. She later took a series of part-time jobs and then a full-time job at a bank when my husband, her youngest, was a teenager.

Unfortunately, she lost the love of her life when he was only fifty-nine. She continued to work and support herself until she retired from the bank a few years later. In addition to losing Charlie at such a young age, she's also lost two of her three children, as well as several siblings. She's battled non-Hodgkin's lymphoma multiple times. But she's come through it all with an amazing spirit and deep religious faith. Today, at eighty-six, she's independent, healthy, and full of great stories about life in the hills and the airplane factory. She's also proud to say she paid her uncle back for that bus ticket.

Evelyn

When World War II began, Evelyn was an eleven-year-old girl living in Germany in a sixteenth century farmhouse with her parents and two sisters. They lived on a large farm in the small, historic town of Fritzlar, which is northeast of Frankfurt. The city is surrounded by a wall and a ring of watchtowers built during medieval times.

Evelyn's father was injured in World War I, so he was not drafted into the German military during the World War II. He didn't belong to the Nazi party, which meant the family was watched closely by the Gestapo and was on a blacklist. Devout Catholics, Evelyn's family continued to attend church, and her father helped a group of Ursuline nuns leave the city after Hitler's regime gave them twenty-four hours to get out. The Nazis frowned upon people who participated in religious activities, but Evelyn's father thought it was worth the risk.

"They (the Gestapo) wrote down the names of everyone who attended church," she said. "Children had to join the Hitler Youth. The meetings were scheduled at the same time as church, so we could not go to church."

By the second year of the war, food was scarce and there was nothing in the stores. Residents were in dire straits. Evelyn's grandmother threw apples and bread across a fence to Jewish neighbors. If she had been caught, she would have suffered greatly for trying to help them.

"The Gestapo counted our animals, and even how many eggs we gathered each day," Evelyn said.

By 1942, bombings began every night at one minute after midnight, and there was no safe place to go. The terror was alive during the day as well. The train Evelyn rode to work was bombed on a regular basis. She described the chaotic scene saying people scrambled for safety by jumping off the train trying to get into ditches or any low spot they could find.

One night stands out in Evelyn's mind all these years later. She distinctly recalls what happened to a nearby town on October 23, 1944. It was a scene straight out of a World War II movie with carnage unlike what most people had ever seen. It was the Americans, however, not the Nazis, who caused it.

"The Americans bombed it, and there were flames as far as you could see," she said. "Eighty percent of the town was destroyed; 23,000 people died. It was hell on Earth."

On Easter morning in 1945, the Americans came to Fritzlar, but the scene was not what many Americans might imagine. General Patton's tanks rolled into the local airport and took it over. Not knowing what awaited them in the town of Fritzlar, the American Army threatened to blow it up if the residents did not surrender.

"Some old men put sheets on big sticks to show we surrendered," she said. "An all-black infantry entered the town. We'd never seen black people before, but we knew they were Americans."

After the war, Germany was in chaos. There was horrible inflation and no government to speak of. Only then did Evelyn's family learn that if Hitler had prevailed, her family would have been sent to Siberia. With her country in such chaos, Evelyn saw no future for herself there.

Luckily, she had family in New York City, so in 1949 Evelyn left Germany for a new life in the United States. A Russian refugee who was part of a group living on the family farm made coats out of blankets for Evelyn and her sisters. When Evelyn stepped off the plane in New York City wearing the blanket coat, her aunt took her immediately to a big department store and bought her a proper coat. Evelyn's youngest daughter still has the coat Evelyn's aunt bought.

"Everything was so plentiful in America," Evelyn said. "I could not believe it."

She went to work in the family's restaurant and bakery, taking care of the books. She spoke English well, but it was Oxford English. Her aunt told her she needed to learn to speak "American." So to work on her American English and further her education, Evelyn enrolled in Columbia University, traveling from Queens to Manhattan by train. After a while, the routine got to be too much and she gave up her classes.

She knew she would not go back to Germany, and she became a US citizen in 1954. She voted in her first presidential election in 1956.

After she'd been in America for about eight years, a voice from the past called her. It was Kurt, her high school sweetheart. When Evelyn decided to come to America, he hadn't wanted to come with her. Instead, he went to Heidelberg to study chemistry. After graduating with a PhD, he was recruited by the US Department of Defense and took a job doing research and teaching at Duke University.

Evelyn began seeing Kurt again, and following a brief courtship, they married in May 1958. She moved with him to Durham, North Carolina, where she was appalled to see the treatment of blacks, Jews, and Catholics.

"New York City is so diverse," she said. "But in the '50s and '60s in the South, there was no diversity. I didn't think that could happen in a democracy like the United States."

All four of Evelyn's children were born in Durham. Although she's proud to be an American, she wanted to preserve some of her German traditions and teach her children the language, so they spoke both English and German in their home. When the oldest child was about nine, Kurt moved the family back to Germany for a short time. He was disappointed in the government and school system he found in his native land, and moved the family back to the US about a year and a half later. He took a job at the University of Kentucky. They finished raising their children in Lexington, and Kurt flourished in his job at the university.

Today, Evelyn is a widow. Her children live in various parts of the US, which has provided Evelyn an opportunity to see more of America and continue studying the history of the country she's called home for more than sixty years.

Linde

Linde also grew up in Germany during World War II, but she is eleven years younger than Evelyn. Although she's never told me many details about that time in her life, I know it had a profound effect on her.

"My most vivid memories are the droning sound of squadrons of bombers overhead at very high altitudes, or if they were flying lower for air raids, the sirens going off and everyone rushing to the basement," she said.

Her family owned a nursery, and Linde and her sisters helped out, but Linde had bigger aspirations. Her dream was to use her multilingual skills as an interpreter at the United Nations.

But as so often happened to young women, that dream was put on hold for marriage and family. In 1957 at age nineteen, she met her future husband, an American military man stationed in Germany. They married in 1958, and she told him she planned to have a career. He agreed to support that plan. But, again fate stepped in and by 1960, when her husband was reassigned to the US, she had two babies.

She and the family moved three times within six years after coming to the states. There was no time for education or a career as Linde moved the family and raised children. She did volunteer work and was very involved at her kids' school. She also became a US citizen in 1964. At that time, she said she had to renounce her allegiance to her native country.

"I never had any reservations about becoming a citizen, saw no reason why I should not, and never had any regrets," she said.

Her husband retired from the military in 1970, and they settled in Lexington, Kentucky, to be close to his family. When Linde's youngest son was old enough to drive, she finally began to pursue her own career. At age forty, after taking a few classes over the years, she enrolled as a full-time college student studying international business. Again, she hoped to use her language skills, but this time in the business world. In the 1970s, however, no global business located in her area would hire her to do anything other than secretarial work, which she soundly rejected.

Disappointed, but not defeated, Linde determined her best course of action was to be self-employed. She and her husband owned some rental property. She'd always had an interest in real estate, so she decided to pursue a career in that field. Linde was extremely successful for a number of years and was a self-employed Realtor until her retirement.

Unfortunately, her husband passed away at age fifty-nine. She said although the death of a spouse is something you never really get over, you come to terms with it.

"Attitude is everything in life," she said. "I don't like to be around negativity."

Her best advice to young women is to get an education and have a financial plan for retirement. Although her retirement years are not what she'd planned with her husband, she's making the best of them. She's still volunteering, has a diverse group of friends, enjoys spending time with her children and grandchildren, and frequently travels to Germany.

Janey

Janey graduated from college in 1971 with a triple major, a high grade point average, and no job prospects. So she went to an employment agency for help. With all she had going for her, you'd think she was very marketable, but she quickly found that wasn't the case.

"I couldn't type seventy words a minute, so they weren't interested in me," she said.

While waiting to speak to an employment counselor Janey struck up conversations with two other people in the lobby. When they told her what types of jobs they were looking for, she proceeded to tell them where they could find openings, and they left. The man who owned the employment agency told one of his employees to get rid of Janey because she was running off all his clients.

A few days later, the agency called to offer her a job as its receptionist, a job that paid minimum wage. She decided minimum wage was better than no wage and took the job. Within a short time, she moved into a counselor position, and in less than a year, the owner, who was in financial difficulty, offered her a partnership.

"He offered me 45 percent of the business," she said. "Even though I'd had no business classes, I knew that wasn't going to work in my favor, so I asked for 50 percent. Because he needed the money, he agreed to it."

One year later she bought him out. But it wasn't easy. She couldn't get a loan in her name even though she made more money than her husband. He still had to co-sign the loan.

Five years later, she added temporary employment services to her offerings through a franchise agreement with a large national firm. It went well for a while, but then she found they had violated the franchise agreement by encroaching on her territory, so she sued. Hundreds of thousands of dollars and more than a year later, she won a bench trial with a precedent-setting verdict on franchise agreements. And she wasn't even thirty years old.

Her business partner told her in 1972 that she'd never succeed because she didn't think big enough. Now, more than forty years later, with BJM Staffing going strong, she's certainly proved him, and a lot of other men, wrong. She also has no trouble getting a loan in her own name.

Rebecca

Rebecca went to college in the mid '60s. When she graduated with a degree in journalism and an internship at a New Orleans television station to her credit, she applied for a job at a small TV station in Florida. She was told that nice young ladies didn't go into journalism. So she went to grad school. After grad school, she began teaching at two universities in the Washington, DC, area.

At nearly twenty-five Rebecca already had accomplished quite a bit, but realized she was the only one of her old high school group who had not married. At the time, it was unusual for a woman to not be married and have a baby or two at that point in her life. Then she met Jonathan at a party at the home of one of her co-workers, and following a brief courtship, Rebecca and Jonathan were married. The marriage produced three children. They were married for seventeen years, but it was not a happy marriage.

Jonathan was an alcoholic and displayed sociopathic behavior. He didn't take care of his family and business obligations. Yet, Rebecca felt somehow his failings were her fault, and that if only she tried hard enough, she could fix the problems with their marriage. But there was one more thing she didn't know, and it was something she couldn't change: Jonathan was gay.

Jonathan had told Rebecca multiple times that he wanted out of the marriage, but never gave her a reason. Rebecca said she suffered from low self-esteem and was willing to do anything she could to keep the marriage together because she had a tremendous fear of abandonment.

When the truth finally came out, two of the couple's kids were in high school and one was in seventh grade. Even with her education and established career, Rebecca still feared she couldn't support the family on her own. She knew there would be little or no help from her soon-to-be ex.

Jonathan had a difficult time admitting to her that he was gay, and Rebecca said he didn't handle the situation well. She said Jonathan told her he'd known since high school that he was gay and had had several affairs over the years.

"At that time, we were taught who you are is not as important as who you should be," Rebecca said.

Her mother-in-law even blamed Rebecca for the break-up, saying it was her "inadequacies" that caused the marriage to fall apart. In reality, Rebecca couldn't have been happier to learn the truth. She wondered if she'd missed the signals, saying maybe her "gaydar" was faulty. But her male gay friends missed those signals, too. None of them had suspected Jonathan was gay.

"I was totally relieved to find out I didn't cause the problems in the marriage," she said. "I kept thinking: thank God it's not my fault."

As surprising as it was to learn she was married to a gay man, Rebecca stressed that Jonathan's sexuality was not the main issue. She could accept that and was glad to learn the truth. The bigger problem in her mind was the dishonesty and sociopathic behavior he displayed during and after the marriage and the toll it took on her children, who had no relationship with their father after the divorce.

A few years ago, Rebecca found out Jonathan had passed away. No one from his family contacted her or her children at the time of his death, and a year had passed before they found out.

Today, in her early sixties, Rebecca is enjoying a great career in consulting. Her three children lead productive lives and her grandchildren are the light of her life. She never remarried.

Tina

Tina, who's now in her late fifties and retired, worked for a utility company her entire career. That's not usual for a lot of people of our generation, particularly those from small towns where good jobs are scarce. She married young and had a child, which also is not unusual for women of that time.

Like most of us, Tina had the desire to progress in her career and make more money. She was a union member, so she had the opportunity to move into higher paying jobs because of her seniority. Gender wasn't supposed to matter. At one point, she bid on and got a job that no woman had had before. But, as the old saying goes, be careful what you wish for. The men she worked with made her life miserable. They compromised her equipment, which also compromised her safety. They sexually harassed her and many other women at the workplace, abuses that were not reported for fear of making things worse. Finally, she'd had enough and bid off the job.

"Even though I belonged to a union, they tried to discriminate against the women when it came to pay, too," she said. "During a strike there was actually talk about paying women less than men for picket line duty."

That time Tina spoke up, but she said many other women kept silent. She continued working for the company because the pay and benefits were good, and in a small town, good jobs are hard to come by. It was also hard to leave because at one point, her husband, sister, and brother-in-law all worked there with her. The camaraderie she had with her female co-workers made going to work more enjoyable. She also played on the company's softball team.

Always an athlete and an avid fitness buff, Tina eventually divorced her husband and married another fitness buff. Life was good until her company announced it was downsizing, and, like many other long-time employees, Tina took a buy-out. She was in her early fifties and not yet ready for retirement. The adjustment wasn't easy.

"It was hard not getting up and going to my job and seeing my friends," she said. "We'd been through everything together—weddings, babies, divorces—and then all of a sudden I wasn't seeing them every day."

She tried other jobs after retirement, but nothing brought her satisfaction. After a few years, she decided she was ready to retire, and now she spends her time enjoying life with her husband and grandchildren. She said even though she doesn't work, she's developed a routine that's helped her adjust to her new life. Having a schedule, even if it's flexible, provides the structure she said she needs to keep motivated. She's also come to view her own value a little differently.

"I don't know why we think we have to work to feel valued," she said. "It's taken me a long time to realize I bring value to my family by the things I do for them, not because of a job or salary."

Mary

When Mary was six years old, she announced that when she grew up she wanted to be an archeologist and go to Egypt and dig up mummies. Her mother told her she thought that was a great idea and would be a very interesting thing to do. Keep in mind this was in Alabama in 1951. Very few women worked and fewer still were archeologists.

Mary's father died in World War II before Mary was born, so her mother moved in with family. Her mother came from a long line of piano teachers, and she followed that path as well. Her schedule followed the school schedule, so when she was off in the summer she took Mary all around the country to visit relatives and to explore.

Two of Mary's favorite places to visit were the Smithsonian in Washington, DC, and the Field Museum in Chicago. She attributes her interest in digging up bones to those early childhood experiences, along with her mother's interest in anthropology and reading.

"She used to read Margaret Mead's column in *Redbook*, and say, 'See, here's a woman who's doing what you want to do,'" Mary said.

After high school Mary attended Birmingham Southern College. She needed to stay close to home because of illness in her family, but this college didn't offer an anthropology major. Instead, Mary majored in English, became involved in theater, and took a class in art history. Because of that class, she decided maybe art history was the way to go. After earning her degree, she did some graduate work in art history but realized her real passion was anthropology. She enrolled in a bio-archeology program at the University of Alabama at Birmingham. She also took a volunteer position and later a paid one with the Arkansas Archeology Survey. She then enrolled in a program at the University of Arkansas and later earned a doctorate at Northwestern University.

For more than twenty years, Mary researched Native American sites in the Southeast and learned she could build a career working on collections that others had dug up years before. During the Great Depression's WPA programs, many sites were excavated as part of dam projects. Most of the artifacts had been packed away but never studied.

Her career included not just studying those collections, but also a variety of digs, working at the Smithsonian, and as the director and curator of the Museum of Anthropology at the University of Kentucky. One of her most exciting projects was also one of her most recent. She spent time in Portugal working on a site that had once been home to a large Roman villa, a church, and two cemeteries. One extraordinary find was a skull she calls the African Queen, which had been dug up in the '70s but never studied.

"I knew it was different from the others and now know she was an African from the fifteenth or sixteenth century," Mary said. "She probably was one of the last people buried at the site, and possibly was a servant or a slave on the big agricultural estate."

Now retired, Mary said she's excavated sites with everything from a dental pick to a back hoe. Although she never worked on a site in Egypt, she's planning a trip there soon.

Phyllis

Sixty-something Phyllis is a feisty redhead who grew up in a coal mining family. By the time she was in seventh grade, her family had moved seven times, which she believes helped her become an outgoing person who makes friends easily.

She graduated from college in 1966 and went to work for the newspaper in the capital city of Frankfort, Kentucky, covering state government. She was paid ninety dollars a week. Shortly thereafter, she got a call asking her to come to work for the newly elected governor as director of the news bureau for the Department of Public Information. She was not the first woman to have the position, but she probably was the youngest.

In 1972, her first husband was offered a job in Atlanta, so the couple moved to Georgia. Phyllis began her job search at the two local papers, but was told because she'd worked in a government public relations position that she could never work in journalism again. Disheartened, she knew she had to look elsewhere. At the time, several advertising agencies were located in one area, so armed with a fist full of résumés she began going door to door. A chance meeting in an elevator led to the next step of her career.

In the elevator, two men looked at her stack of résumés and asked what she was doing. As she explained about her job search, she handed them a copy of her résumé. A quick glance at it told them all they needed to know. They worked for an agency that had been hired to help the Georgia House of Representatives find its first public information officer, and now they'd found her by accident on an elevator.

The Georgia governor at the time was Jimmy Carter, and the House of Representatives included a young man named Julian Bond, who would become known nationally as the leader of the National Association for the Advancement of Colored People (NAACP). Although Phyllis did not work directly with the governor, she did get to know Bond.

Phyllis worked in the Georgia House position for a few years and then decided to return home without her soon-to-be ex-husband. After returning to Kentucky in 1976, Phyllis once again went to work in the state capital at the Kentucky Chamber of Commerce and the Legislative Research Commission. She also worked on political campaigns.

In 1981, she took her government relations skills in a new direction and began working as a lobbyist for IBM and later Lexmark. After her retirement from Lexmark, Phyllis went back into state government offices and worked for the Commerce Cabinet and Kentucky Senate. She also opened a children's clothing store, called Miss P's Kids, which keeps her busy these days. She continues to keep confidences and provide counsel to many people inside and outside of government.

"My life has been a series of accidents that always seemed to turn out well," she said. "And I'd highly recommend looking for a job in an elevator."

One more thing of note: Even though she couldn't work as a journalist in Atlanta, Phyllis became president of the Atlanta Press Club and served two terms. It was her way of saying, "Take that, Mr. Editor."

Joan

Born in 1930, Joan is a youthful, fun-loving, African-American woman who saw discrimination firsthand. She's also a twenty-two-year pancreatic cancer survivor.

As a little girl, Joan lived with a foster family because her mother was a live-in cook for wealthy white families. She said it was a happy childhood, growing up with older foster sisters, and she saw her mother frequently. She attended segregated schools, which got leftover books and gym equipment when the local schools for whites replaced theirs.

At the age of twelve, she took her first train ride to Dayton, Ohio, where her mother worked for an Air Force officer and his family.

"I had to change trains in Cincinnati, and I couldn't wait to explore that train station," she said.

But it was not to be. Her mother had made arrangements for Travelers' Aid to babysit Joan and make sure she got on the right train to Dayton. So even though her mother was not always there, she made sure Joan was always safe.

Joan's experiences growing up in Lexington, Kentucky, were similar to what blacks in many other parts of the country recall. The city was segregated in every way. Whites lived in one part of town; blacks in another. There were separate business districts, too. Whites never went into the black area and didn't allow black people in most of their businesses.

Joan recalls not being allowed to eat in downtown Lexington restaurants or to shop in most stores. African-American men, however, were allowed to shop in many stores but couldn't try on the clothes. There were very few movie theaters where black people were allowed entrance. Where they were allowed, black people entered in the back, bought their tickets from a black woman, and had to sit in a balcony five flights up. One of the theaters where blacks were not allowed is still open today, but Joan said she hasn't forgotten what it used to be like.

"There wasn't a sign or anything saying we couldn't go in, but we knew," she said. "I still won't go in there."

When Joan was nineteen, her mother worked for a woman who rented a summer home in Rhode Island. The employer allowed Joan to go with her mother and help in the kitchen. It was quite an experience for a young woman of that time.

"We rode the train and had to sit in the back," she said. "When we got to Ashland (Kentucky), we were allowed to sit anywhere, enter the dining car, and have a sleeping berth. That was very surprising to me."

That summer, as World War II raged on, Joan's mother and the other domestic help did their part to help ease the suffering of a few German families. The employer's chauffer and two childcare workers were German. With the grease Joan's mother saved from the kitchen, the Germans made soap, which they sent to family in Germany. They also sent clothing and other items they could scrounge.

Although Joan had hoped to go to nursing school, she couldn't afford it. So she moved to western Kentucky to attend a vocational training school and became a cosmetologist.

In 1954, Joan married Joe, a man she'd known most of her life. He'd served in the Air Force during the Korean War and qualified for a GI Loan to pay for college. By that time, blacks were allowed to attend the University of Kentucky. Joe enrolled in the engineering program in 1955, becoming the first black man to do so.

Later that year, Joan had a son. While her husband attended school, it meant lean times for the little family. In addition to working as a cosmetologist, Joan took in washing and ironing to help make ends meet.

"I did whatever I could to bring in money, and my husband worked when he could," she said. "You have to have faith, and you can't give up."

Their sacrifice paid off when Joe graduated with a degree in electrical engineering and a 3.8 grade point average. Still, in certain parts of the county, some companies were not interested in hiring a black electrical engineer. Joe eventually was hired by the Philadelphia Naval Air Development Center, and the family moved north, where they lived for thirty years.

During that time, Joan worked at a hospital, and in 1989, she was diagnosed with pancreatic cancer. After a long, hard road to recovery, she and Joe moved back to Lexington to be near aging parents. Their son stayed in Philadelphia and now has his own family.

Sadly, Joe passed away, but in 2007, he was honored posthumously by UK's College of Engineering Hall of Distinction. He earned six patents and had a distinguished career.

"I appreciate all we went through," Joan said. "It made us better people—maybe better than some others."

Anita

Anita didn't plan to be a lawyer, but she became a well-respected one. After graduating from college and working a couple of years, it became clear to her that something was going to have to change. She needed to make more money because she had to take care of her parents.

"I'm not from a family of lawyers, and when I told folks I was going to law school, they said, 'good luck with that,'" she said.

When Anita started law school in 1979, only seven of the 100 graduates at her law school that year were women. By the time she graduated in 1982, the number had climbed to about 30 percent. She said the male students had no problem with their female cohorts, but some of the faculty did. Only two members of the faculty were female, and Anita said it was clear that some of the male faculty were uncomfortable having female students.

After graduation, Anita went to her first job interview with high expectations. She loved horses and wanted to work in equine law. So, like any good law student, she found the most successful equine attorney in the state and landed an interview. He was very late, but she said that didn't bother her because she wanted the job so badly.

"The first question he asked was if I was married," she said. "I knew that was illegal to ask, but I just answered, 'No, sir.' He then said, 'That's good because judges don't like little girl lawyers who have to go home and cook supper.' My response was, 'That won't be a problem because I don't cook.'" The interview went downhill from there.

Not long after, she landed a job with another firm. Anita has several stories about being mistaken for a male colleague's secretary, court reporter, or a paralegal. She was called "that little girl from Lexington" by a judge in another county. But she thinks things have turned around for women in the law today.

"Women are at the top in most areas of practice," she said. "There's still a pay disparity, but I'd say that's because there aren't equal opportunities. Most of the time, men control the flow of work, and men reach out to other men for help. There are a lot of reasons for that. Some of it is just a comfort level for them."

She's frustrated by what she sees in some younger female attorneys, too. Anita says they want to be at the top, but aren't always willing to do what it takes to get there after Anita and other women have blazed the trail for them. "I've been driving a backhoe for years," she said.

Anita also said some younger women don't fully appreciate what she and other female attorneys of her generation faced. "The younger women, they've never been called a 'little girl lawyer' or asked if they can type," she said. "They've been on par from the get-go and expect to progress and be compensated the same whether they do the same work or not."

Anita worked for a large firm for many years, but she recently struck out on her own with a couple of female partners. They focus primarily on family law. Although she doesn't practice equine law, she still loves horses and rides as often as she can. She's also developed into quite the cook, but has never had to leave court early to make dinner.

Patricia

At some time in their lives, many Catholic girls consider becoming a nun. Patricia did, too, but only after her husband passed away and her children were grown. As unusual as that may sound, it's not unheard of. Here's what led to her decision and the path she followed.

When Patricia and Joe married, she was nineteen and he was thirty. Even though there was a big age difference and their backgrounds were very different, it was a good marriage. They had three children and a good life until Joe became ill.

Although he'd seen several doctors, they were unable to diagnose Joe's problem. Finally, they had an answer: a pancreatic tumor. He had surgery at Mayo Clinic, but he and the family knew that because of the location of the tumor, it was mostly inoperable. During Joe's illness Patricia was working, but Joe was unable to and the family would have fallen on hard times if it had not been for the generosity of fellow parishioners, friends, and family.

"Anonymously, people left money in our mailbox," she said. "Once, a policeman dropped off bags and bags of groceries."

The family felt blessed, and in light of his faith, Joe was humbled and moved to tears by this outpouring of generosity. Patricia said Joe wished he had been more generous to others in need when he was able. For Patricia, the experience created a spiritual awakening.

"These were our angels," she said. "They lived their faith."

Unfortunately, Joe didn't make it and when he passed away, it left a big hole in the family's life. The kids were in college, high school, and middle school. Patricia was only thirty-eight. Eight months after Joe's death, she attended a spiritual retreat. She said she hadn't cried or grieved because she still felt his presence, but in a different way.

"I had a spiritual experience in the garden at the retreat," she said. "I felt that Joe was there with me."

A year later, she felt called to live a holy life, but it was too soon to commit to that. Her children had not begun to heal from the loss of their father and were not ready to lose their mother to a cloistered order of nuns. But fifteen years later, after much thought and preparation, Patricia made the move.

"I sold the house," she said. "I didn't want to own things. There's freedom in that."

She moved to Chicago where she lived in community with the Sisters of St. Francis while she worked through the process of determining if her vocation would be permanent. The first year she had freedom to intern in an urban clinical pastoral education program and work with formerly homeless mothers and their children.

The next stage was much more difficult. She had only fifteen days that year in which she was allowed to be apart from the community. She determined the life of a vowed religious was not the right direction for her life, but she was invited to stay another year.

"It was the best year of my life," Patricia said. "I wrote for therapy. I went back to Rochester (Minnesota) and talked with the chaplain who was on the Mayo Clinic staff when Joe was there. I re-lived that process and finally cried."

Patricia realized she was living a holy life and didn't have to take vows to prove it. Today, she remains associated with the Sisters of St. Francis. She's highly involved and a founding member of the Franciscan

Peace Center, which develops interfaith programs. The organization envisions and believes in a nonviolent way of life that will bring about a peaceful global community.

"I don't know that there's one answer for everyone," she said. "I'm an optimistic person and believe it's important to enjoy life and to be open to what it has to offer."

Susan

Many of us know stories about women who give up who they are to make someone else, usually a spouse or significant other, happy. So how does a strong person who knows herself become insecure and accommodating, lose her dreams, and eventually find her way back? That's Susan's story.

Susan always wanted a good marriage and children, but those things didn't come her way when she thought they would. She hoped she'd meet the right person in college, but it didn't happen. After earning a degree in psychology, Susan moved back to her hometown but couldn't find a job. Eventually, she took a job with the IRS as a tax collector in Appalachia, following up unanswered collection letters with home visits.

"I was young and naïve and didn't think about the danger," she said. "Here I was, this little blonde girl, knocking on doors in remote areas. They probably thought I was the Avon lady as they answered the door with a smile. Then I'd flip out my FBI-like identification and the smile would change to a look of surprise."

Her dad told her to stick it out for a year and try to get transferred from the field to a position in the training group. After four years and countless tears, the transfer had not come.

She decided her only way out was to go back to school. So off she went to the University of Georgia to earn a master's degree in business. She was awarded an assistantship as director of the graduate and international residence hall. Even though it was a tough adjustment living in a dorm in her late twenties, Susan once again turned her challenges into achievements and was very successful at UGA.

After a brief stint in software sales and marketing, Susan moved home to care for her mother, who had lymphoma. She eventually landed her ideal job as the president of the local Junior Achievement office, which encompassed programs in three states. At age forty, she still hadn't met her Prince Charming, and her inner entrepreneur was struggling to get out. So, she left JA after several successful years and briefly started a clothing business. Shortly thereafter, she met a nice guy, gave up her business and took another safe job with a government-funded program called School to Careers. When the grant funding for that program expired a year and a half later, she considered going back to school for another master's degree—this time in counseling.

By now she was married. Maybe he wasn't Mr. Right, but he seemed right at the time and her biological clock was ticking. Before the marriage, her husband agreed to have a child even though he had a teenager from another marriage. When the time came to follow through, he balked at starting a new family in his forties. He didn't see the value in her pursuit of yet another degree either. She'd been accepted into the counseling program with a full scholarship, but she backed out at the last minute because of her husband's objections, naively sacrificing another piece of her dreams to honor the wishes of a significant other.

"I allowed my husband's opinions to make me doubt myself," she said. "It was the first step down the road to losing touch with my inner voice."

She gave up her dream of having children and earning her counseling degree, and took yet another government job, this time with the Veteran's

Administration processing claims amidst a maze of file cabinets and cubicles. After four days, she knew it wasn't a good fit.

"I felt my creative spirit being suffocated," Susan said. "My husband encouraged me to try it for a year. So I toughed it out, telling myself that maybe it would get better. I stopped listening to my own heart."

After four years, she left the VA and got certified to become a life coach. At the same time, she started renovating a home that she planned to use as an office. Her marriage was going downhill fast. When it finally ended, Susan moved into the renovated home and had found a new career, but it wasn't as a life coach. She began buying older homes to update and re-sell. After years of watching HGTV and attending Sunday afternoon open house real estate showings, Susan had finally found her calling.

"I decided to take control of my life," she said. "I started spending more time with positive people and began to feel more calm, peaceful, and powerful."

At this writing, Susan has flipped four homes, making a nice profit on each. She said it hasn't been easy and that she's made mistakes. She's also been down to her last few dollars along the way.

"A lot of people couldn't live this way," she said. "But I feel like I'm really living my life now, not just going through the motions to build up a retirement plan. I enjoy getting up in the morning and have this sense that it's going to be OK."

Eddie

Edna, known as Eddie, grew up in Georgia at a time when she said there were societal rules and people followed them. Women dressed appropriately in public. Unwed women who found themselves in the family way were not celebrated. Men took care of their families and women took care of the children and home. Although those were the rules, it didn't mean everyone liked them.

"Mother wanted to work, but my father wouldn't allow it," Eddie said.

Unlike a lot of young ladies in the early 1950s, Eddie went to college. But like many others who went, she didn't finish because she met her future husband, Frank, and they married in 1952.

"I was just a freshman when we met," she said. "He was six years older than me and was going to college on the GI bill."

They bought a three-bedroom starter home complete with a dishwasher. "Dishwashers and washing machines were supposed to make life easier," she said. "But they just created more demand on us because people thought we had more free time."

After she'd been married for nine months, Eddie's mother-in-law told her it was now OK to have a baby. Eddie and Frank eventually had four daughters.

It was a traditional 1950s lifestyle straight out of *Leave It to Beaver*.

In the evening, Eddie fixed a nice meal for dinner, dressed appropriately, and had a martini waiting for Frank when he came in from work.

Frank's job took them from Georgia to Ohio to Florida, and finally to Kentucky, where he started his own business. Eddie always had interests outside the home and several times considered getting a job. But like her father, Eddie's husband didn't want his wife to work.

As things within his industry started to change and Frank approached sixty-five, he decided to sell the business and retire.

"My daughters worried about him retiring and being home with me all day," Eddie said.

Unbeknownst to Frank and her daughters, Eddie had that covered. When Frank retired, she went to work. She was fifty-nine when she landed her first full-time job. She'd always had an interest in home decorating, so Eddie took a job in the home department of a department store.

"I didn't tell him I was going to do it," she said. "I just did it. I had had enough of staying at home."

That's when something interesting began to happen at home—a complete role reversal occurred. Frank learned to cook and had the martinis ready when Eddie came in from work.

"He got good at certain things," Eddie said. "He made good spaghetti sauce and fried chicken."

He also vacuumed and did other household chores that he'd never done before. He worked in the garden and the yard and made the most of his retirement. Eddie finally decided to retire at age seventy-three. Sadly, Frank passed away just one year later.

"Fifty must be a turning point," she said. "I was really tired of staying home and did something about it. I think the fifties are just a great time in life."

April

Growing up in a New Jersey suburb, April never imagined living the life she has today. She was born in Queens, and when she was six, April's family moved across the bridge to New Jersey. Her father, a musician, commuted daily to Manhattan. Her mother was a homemaker and political activist for many years. When April's parents divorced her mother went into real estate with a focus on fair housing.

"I learned a lot about activism and grunt work," April said. "I remember riding a bus to see Martin Luther King give his 'I have a dream' speech. I didn't really know who he was or what it was all about."

As a teenager, April loved motorcycles and fast cars. She said she wasn't much of a student but was first in her industrial arts class.

"I had a knack for fixing things," she said. "I remember the first time I fixed the car. We were on the way to the beach, and going to the beach was very important to me."

April's first job was pumping gas. She wanted to be a machinist, but there were no jobs for young women in that field in the '70s. She saw an ad for a locksmith trainee and checked it out. At first, the woman who co-owned the business with her husband was not encouraging. But after she noticed April's birthday was the same as her own, the woman decided to give April a chance.

This job started April down a path toward meeting a man who

would eventually change her life. She continued working as a locksmith and eventually became a safe and vault expert. In 1983, she decided to take a locksmith certification course.

"I was late, and arrived on my motorcycle, and was completely inappropriately dressed," she said.

She didn't know at the time what the instructor thought of her, but she was interested in him immediately. Clay worked for the lock company his father started and traveled around the country teaching certification classes. In time, a courtship began between April and Clay.

About a year later, she moved to the small, rural area in Kentucky where Clay's father's business was located, and she went to work for the company as the director of education. Clay continued traveling and teaching certification classes. In addition to their day jobs, April and Clay bought a trade magazine and eventually started the Safe and Vault Technicians Association.

In 1987, Clay surprised April with a gift—one that she said had not been appropriately discussed. He brought home a long-tailed macaque that he'd purchased from an exotic pet dealer in another state. The couple already had birds and other animals, but Gizmo the monkey had completely different needs.

"He joined our household and changed our lives forever," April said.

Because they knew so little about monkeys, the couple began trying to learn as much as they could about primates as pets. This was before the Internet, so finding information was not easy. What they were learning was not good, and they knew pretty quickly they had a problem. One of the first things they learned was that Gizmo needed social enrichment. They found another monkey owner close by that had discovered monkey ownership was not for him, so he gave them his monkey. Now, Gizmo had a new friend and April had double trouble.

The more April learned about having primates as pets, the more convinced she was that it was a mistake. She learned about experimental labs, exotic pet dealers, and exotic pet auctions. April still tears up talking about the first time she saw a chimp being auctioned. She was certain chimps were endangered and not allowed to be sold. Unfortunately, she learned of a loophole in the law that allows chimps to be imported for research. Many chimps are sold as pets even though they've been brought to the US legally.

As she learned more about the seedy world of exotic pet sales, April and Clay tried to figure out how to stop them. By this time, she was becoming known for her activism and asked to consider taking in some chimps from a lab that was closing in New York.

"I never wanted chimps," April said. "They're huge, and I was scared to work with them."

But what she saw at the lab were baby chimps in a nursery, and a short time later, April and Clay brought eight of them back to Kentucky. They thought they could care for the small animals, but were misled about the amount of care that was needed. They also realized they were going to have to create a nonprofit organization for this sanctuary they'd accidently created on the site they purchased for building a weekend home.

"We had to have a plan because we knew they were going to outlive us," she said. "With good care, chimps could live to be sixty or seventy years old."

One of the original eight chimps died soon after arriving at the sanctuary, but the other seven are thriving along with a group of older chimps April rescued from Georgia several years later. Now with 50 residents, including a variety of monkeys and the chimps, the Primate

Rescue Center is a place to behold. Along with an indoor area for the chimps, there's a large outdoor enclosure so they can live as normally as possible. Gizmo still lives at the sanctuary and soon will be 25 years old.

April continues to advocate for chimps and other primates all around the country. She belongs to a group of sanctuary owners and frequently is seen on national and local television reminding people that primates and other exotic animals are not suitable as pets.

Jo

Jo was a shy child who had few friends, but she believed anything was possible. Her father was a doctor, so at age fourteen, Jo got her first job at a hospital as a nursing assistant in labor and delivery. Deciding a health care career was not for her, she went on to have many years of success in television, diplomatic service, and public relations. But as she got close to fifty, Jo found herself unemployed for the first time. She was angry, frustrated, and concerned about her future.

Over the next several months as she looked for a job, Jo became painfully aware there were few positions available, and she was overqualified for the ones she found. Younger supervisors were not interested in having a subordinate who knew more than they did. Plus, Jo wanted a job that would interest and challenge her, not just a paycheck. In the back of her mind, she'd been considering turning her hobby into a business, and the lack of good jobs in her field led her to decide to move in a new direction.

For years, Jo had trained service dogs mainly for assisting children with autism. She had not charged for her services because she loved dogs and helping people. While unemployed, she began to wonder if she could turn dog training into a full-time career. She started the process of setting up a nonprofit entity and became certified by the American Kennel Club. She soon realized the economy not only had taken a toll on her options for a public relations job, but it also had curtailed spending on dog training. She learned, however, that the dog grooming business was still robust and profitable. So she enrolled in a dog grooming class and began talks with a local groomer about taking a position there when she finished her classes.

"It's so weird to be at this point in my career," she said. "I feel like I'm starting my career in reverse order."

Her career reads like a dream. She worked in London for the BBC, then as a producer at CNN for sixteen years. Jo landed interviews with people like King Hussein of Jordan, Henry Kissinger, General Norman Schwarzkopf, and Ross Perot. She'd heard that most of these men were difficult to get interviews with, but she succeeded in landing them by taking advantage of her Southern upbringing.

"I learned that being a Southern woman using charm and a gentle manner, you can push people without them knowing they're being pushed," she said.

One of her biggest success stories was interviewing a man in Jordan about a so-called honor killing. His sixteen-year-old sister had been raped, and he said he killed her to restore honor to the family. Although this practice was prevalent, Jo was able get King Hussein to condemn it in her interview with him. In addition to the story itself being a huge coup, Jo said she knew she'd done well when her story was followed by one exactly like it by Diane Sawyer.

After leaving CNN, Jo took a job with the British consulate as vice consul of press and public affairs. She had that position for five years. During that time she met her future husband, a robotics engineer. She chucked the glamorous life in Atlanta and moved to a rural area in another state. Between them, they had six children from their previous marriages, so her small family was now a large one.

After moving to a state with fewer appropriate job opportunities, Jo took a job with a local university. She used her experience with the

British Consulate and her travel in the Middle East to land a job with the university's Homeland Security training program. The position was funded by a grant, so when the funding was close to an end, Jo looked for another position. She found one in a quasi-governmental organization. It turned out to be the one that ended badly.

"Your job defines you," she said. "My husband thought unemployment was harder for men until he saw what I've gone through. Going to the unemployment office is humiliating."

Even though Jo is still struggling with her job loss and career transition, she sees a future in dog grooming and training. The best part of her new career was finding that she could be relaxed even though she's working.

"After spending my life in stressful situations, dog grooming is so relaxing, and I have something beautiful when I'm done," she said. "The training is very rewarding."

Jo believes you can reinvent yourself if you have to. She said she's taken things she's learned at each job and transferred them to other jobs. She believes people's attitude and approach create the outcomes they have in life. Her attitude is, if adversity is staring you in the face, it isn't signaling the end. It's a new beginning.

"For all the stuff I've done, I feel like I should be one hundred, not fifty," she said. "I've travelled on whaling vessels, tracked tigers in India, joined border patrol on midnight round-up in California, and ridden an elephant in a circus. I've shaken hands with world leaders, helped a former president get health kits to war-torn African nations, and had tea with royalty. Now I've literally gone to the dogs and started over at fifty!"

Conclusion

So what did all of this research tell us? Well, several things. Women over fifty *are* more than N/A, as my friend Jan said. We're working women, retirees, wives, mothers and grandmothers, work-out enthusiasts, gardeners, readers, ladies who lunch, volunteers, and good friends. We're not invisible, although some restaurant servers might want us to be because we're loud when we get together in groups.

Contrary to conventional wisdom, we're not all searching for our lost youth or trying to reinvent ourselves after retirement. Some are, and that's OK. Perhaps most surprising was that the majority of the women who took my survey said they think they look good for their age. We're a happy, realistic group that is, for the most part, content and at peace. Another surprise for me was that more than half of the survey participants said they felt the best is yet to come for them.

We have myriad concerns. Most of our worries are about our children, grandchildren, the state of the world, our health as we age, having enough money to retire, and making our money last after retirement. We want younger women to learn from us. The big take away from this question was that younger women should get a good education and establish their financial independence. We also want them to try new things, stress less about the small stuff and enjoy life.

I've also learned that some of the older women profiled have survived a lot, and they're still kickin'. Those of us in our fifties and sixties can learn from them the qualities of perseverance, courage, and optimism. Also, they show us that getting older doesn't mean we have to slow down or be relegated to an easy chair. They are vibrant, busy women who enjoy life to the fullest.

Here are some other things I've learned in my fifty-plus years that the book research didn't tell me:

- After reaching a certain age, bags under your eyes don't go away unless a plastic surgeon is involved. Ditto the turkey neck.

- Black *is* slimming.

- Hair color is my friend.

- Horseback riding is not as easy as it looks.

- Life is about choices. We all make some good and some bad ones.

- I'll never again look like I did at twenty, thirty, or even forty. The most I can do is try to look my best for the age I am.

- It's not healthy to live in the past.

- Most women, no matter what their age, don't have the arms for sleeveless clothes but they wear them anyway.

- Most people don't look at their backside in the mirror before they leave home.

- Designers don't make clothes for women my age.

- At some point, cleavage is no longer sexy. It's just saggy. And, oh yeah, unless you're a Hooters' girl, it's never appropriate at work.

- If shoes aren't comfortable when you try them on, they aren't ever going to be.

- Men like to shop at home improvement stores.

- Marriage works best when your husband is your best friend.

- Being a mom is hard no matter what the age of the child.

- If there's a child in a restaurant, it will cry or shriek. Most likely its parents will ignore it.

- Even though people assure you they will keep a secret, most won't.

- Buying a car is excruciating.

- Money isn't the most important thing in life, but it sure makes life easier.

- Life's too short to be unhappy. We only get one life, so we have to make the most of it.

Appendix

Online Survey Demographics

The online survey was conducted via Survey Monkcy between December 2009 and February 2010. It was sent to sixty-three women in three states who were asked to take the survey and forward it to friends and relatives.

Respondents

264 from 24 states

Age

50-59: 58%
60-69: 32%
70-79: 9%
80-89: 1%

Work Status

Full-time: 59%
Part-time: 15%
Retired: 25%
Never worked outside the home: 2 respondents

Marital Status

Married: 71%

Divorced: 18%

Widowed: 8%

Never married: 3%

Multiple Choice Questions

(Percentages are rounded so some categories may not equal 100.)

1. How happy would you say you are?

Very happy: 41%

Happy most of the time: 54%

Not very happy or unhappy: 4%

2. Would you describe yourself as:

Optimistic. I look for the best in everything and everyone: 45%

Realistic. Sometimes things happen and I just deal with it: 53%

Pessimistic. If something bad is going to happen, it will happen to me: 1%

3. If you have grandchildren, how big a part of your life have they become?

Very big. I see or talk to them often: 31%

I'm somewhat involved, but am busy with a variety of things: 14%

Not very big: 4%

I don't have grandchildren: 51%

4. What role do friends play in your life?

They're very important to me: 80%

They're somewhat important, but I don't have time to see them: 18%

They aren't a priority in my life: 3%

5. Excluding co-workers, how often do you see or talk with close friends?

Every day/most days: 30%

Weekly: 50%

Every 4-6 weeks: 14%

A few times a year: 6%

6. How important is your faith as you go about your daily life?

Very important: 66%

Somewhat important: 25%

Not very important: 6%

Unimportant: 4%

7. How often do you attend religious services?

Often: 52%

Occasionally: 20%

Rarely: 19%

Never: 10%

8. What do you think most days when you look in the mirror?

I look good: 26%

I look OK for my age: 62%

I look old and tired: 13%

9. How do you feel most days?

Great: 44%

OK: 52%

Not so good: 3%

10. Do you exercise and try to eat a healthy diet?

Yes. Most of the time: 47%

I try to but am not very disciplined: 42%

I rarely exercise and usually eat whatever I want: 12%

11. How has your weight changed since you were 35?

I weigh less: 6%

I weigh about the same: 20%

I've gained at least 10 pounds: 23%

I've gained nearly 20 pounds: 20%

I've gained more than 20 pounds: 31%

12. I feel as if:

I've reached the high point of my life and am on the downside: 18%

I'm treading water trying to decide what to do with the next chapter
of my life: 35%

The best is yet to come: 48%

Open-ended questions

Top categories of answers are listed.

How is your life different now than it was 20 years ago?

Many are divorced, widowed, or remarried

More health problems or less energy

Wiser, more content, less stressed and happier

Empty nesters, have more time for themselves

What motivates you, or what do you look forward to?

Spending time with family and friends

Faith, spirituality, God

Travel

Helping others

Fitness/exercise

Work, earning money

Retirement

As we get older, friends and family members suffer from illness and some pass away. How do you keep a positive outlook amid all the bad news?

Have learned to accept death and keep moving forward

Focus on the positive

Faith, belief in God, prayer, meditation

Excluding the state of today's economy, what worries you?

Health, getting older, lifelong financial independence, don't want to
  be a burden

Children's future

Environment, crime, nuclear arms, terrorism, state of the world

US government, politics

Dumbing down of America, what the future generation believes is
  important

What advice would you give to younger women?

Get an education, follow your dreams, be financially independent and
  self-reliant

Eat healthy and exercise

Take time for yourself, be true to yourself

Stay positive, enjoy life, don't sweat the small stuff

Enjoy your children while they're young

Acknowledgments

This book never could have been written without the help of the hundreds of women who participated in the online survey and one-on-one interviews. Thanks so much to all of you who took time to give your views and tell your stories. I also appreciate all the women who connected me with their mothers and friends.

Thanks go out to my friends who pushed me to do this and to those who kept me on my toes by asking when the book would be finished. Special thanks to Gale Clarke and Doris Derifield who kept nudging until I took the first step.

Thanks also to Carla VanHoose for reviewing and analyzing the research and to Susan Lindsey for editing. I have to thank my mom, Joan Musser, and my brother, Jim Musser, for supporting me all along the way. And thanks to Bradley, my son, who helped me gather information from restaurant servers.

Last but not least, thank you to Terry, my husband, who dealt with all my angst about writing and publishing. Unfortunately, he won't be able to retire on sales from this book and neither will I. But writing a book and getting it published is something we talked about for years, and now it's done.

About the Author

Mary Hemlepp is a fifty-something public relations consultant. She's an avid reader who always thought she'd write a great mystery novel but decided they're easier to read than to write. She has an adult son and lives in Lexington, Kentucky, with her husband, Terry.